WORKING THE WORDS

BY

JEFFREY DEAN DOTY

WORKING THE WORDS

BY

JEFFREY DEAN DOTY

DEDICATION

For Marie Doty, who taught me to love the written
word.

FOREWORD

There is no magic formula that I, or any other author, can give you for writing the perfect book. Let's just get that out of the way right here and now. What I can give you is a few tools to help you along the way. Some insights into both writing, and the writing life. I am an author, a journalist, and an editor. I have been teaching other writers for over fifteen years now, both in workshops and one-on-one mentoring. I have come up with essays over that time that address the most frequent problems for writers. The handbook you are looking at now is a collection of those essays and a few lessons from my workshops.

This is not a vast and ponderous tome that illuminates every aspect of writing, but a slim guide to get you past the common difficulties without having to wade through endless pages of confusing rules and metaphorical instructions. It is intended to be one part clear cut instruction, and two parts straight forward encouragement.

I am keeping everything as short and to the point as possible to reduce any confusion and increase clarity. This is meant to be a handbook, a basic guide. It is meant to give you some ideas, some paradigms about how writing works. If only one thing you discover in this handbook changes the way you write for the better, and I believe it will, then it is worth the reading.

At any rate, I have tried my best to give you some good information, and a solid understanding of the purpose behind fiction writing, if not a magic formula that makes it all simple. Please write and let me know if you ever find that magic formula—I'd pay good money for it!

J.D.D.

January 22, 2014

WHY WE WRITE

For each of us who write, the reason we do it is different. I've known writers who do it out of an angry desire to rage at the universe. There are those who put down words in an effort to come to terms with the world around them. Some want to be heard. Others want to scratch a creative itch inside them that will come out no other way. Some write to impress or gain lovers. But the only real reason to write, the one underlying all the rest, is because you must.

If you are drawn back to the blank page time and time again, even though wrestling the words loose from your brain and putting them down is an agony of frustration. Or if you look at what you've written in despair, seeing flaws and mediocrity everywhere, but that one shining line you got just right, the one turn of phrase that is perfection, is enough to bring you back tomorrow to suffer the agonies once more… why then, you are writing for the right reason: the magic is in you. You may not be very good at it just yet, but the calling is strong enough to pull you along until you are.

The whole motivating force behind writing is the desire to communicate a small piece of ourselves to the universe at large. I believe this is to make up for our personal issues. Many of us are introverts, some are neurotic, some are loud and rude, others are insecure to a fault, but the blank page is the great redeemer; we are all gods when we write.

Think of it! When you type the first line of your novel, you begin to create a world that does not exist, and then you call forth people to bring life to your world. This is power of a kind only wielded by the Creator. You dream up characters, flesh them out with habits, speech patterns, idiosyncrasies, fears, dreams, and hopes. You throw tragedies, obstacles, and hardships at these individuals you have created in an effort to shape them, teach them lessons, and find out exactly what they are made of. You control the weather, the setting, the ebb and flow of the tides, and even the phases of the moon. You can create a chair, a room, a house, a neighborhood, a city, a country, a world, a star system, or even a universe. You are only limited by the scope of your imagination. And the story is all yours, a precious part of what is inside you, and when you publish, you're releasing your soul into the wind to be carried to the four corners of the Earth.

There are some serious risks and rewards to doing this. First of all, you risk criticism from an uncaring world. Christopher Hampton sums it up well when he says, "Asking a writer what he thinks about critics is like asking a lamp-post how it feels about dogs." When you read that first cutting critique of a story you have come to love like it is your child, you will be surprised at the depth of hurt and anger that wells up inside you. You will eventually learn to be at peace with this, and accept that you cannot please everyone, but it will not be an easy process.

As for rewards, there is nothing so satisfying as seeing your book sell, even if it is not rocketing to the top of the bestseller list. And most surprising, and humbling, is when you discover copies of your book are being bought overseas. With the digital book market, this will happen. I recently learned that one of my books was selling better overseas than it was at home in the United States. Imagine my shock when I saw copies had sold in Brazil—I've never even dreamed of going to Brazil and people there are reading my work!

Fan letters are awesome. More so than critical acclaim or monetary rewards, fan letters validate your writing, for they mean your words connected with someone and moved them so deeply they needed to reach out and tell you. My first fan letter came from a young boy who'd read my story, *Dragon Treat*, in *Cricket Magazine*, and he wrote the magazine to tell them how much he liked my story. Cricket sent the message on to me. It was a simple letter, not gushing, just a statement that he enjoyed the story and wanted to see more like it. It amazed me. I felt like Sally Field at the Oscars crying, "You like me! You really like me!" I understand completely how joyfully surprised she felt in that moment.

It takes years of effort to get to the point where your writing will move readers. It takes patience, determination, and a resilience of spirit. You will spend countless hours reading, studying other writers' techniques, learning, and endless more hours of writing before your own natural style emerges and you begin to find success in print. The odd thing is that you wouldn't miss any of it, because as your writing begins to truly flow through you, the words attain a life of their own, and they draw you into your own world as though you were a passenger, rather than the driver, of your story.

For many of us, the desire to communicate will change into a desire to communicate *better*! That is what will carry you in the future; the belief that you can do better. There will always be one more story in you. One more chance to write the great novel. One more chance to get it right, start to finish!

Think about all that you want to say to the world. Don't you really want to scream, "I'm here! I *matter*!" to the universe? If you say it right, the universe will listen… and you will be a writer.

WHAT IT'S ALL ABOUT

Many writers know what they want to write. They want to write a love story, an adventure, a mystery, a memoir, or a true crime novel. They know what genre their story will fall into. They may even know how they want to write this blossoming novel; they've chosen a style and point of view. However, many of them don't understand what it's all about. They don't know the whole focus of a story is to put the reader into the Dream State.

The Dream State is what, as writers, we must induce in our readers in order to move them and engage them fully in our stories. The Dream State is the experience you get when you turn the last page of a book with complete dread because you don't want the story to end. In the Dream State you hear the chuff of breath from an impatient horse, you feel the slick-smooth texture of satin against your fingertips, you smell the acrid, choking fumes of a chemical fire, you see the tiny rip in the red vinyl seat cover on the cross-town bus, and you taste the salty sweat on a lover's neck in the heat of a July night. All we have for tools to create this experience with is words, but the right words, the tiny details, the sensory input, all come together to create the immersive dream in the reader's mind. It is so much more than a movie, because if the imagination is engaged, and then properly fed on a steady stream of sensory input in just the right amount, the reader will not only see and hear it, they will LIVE it! For them it will be as if they are in the room with your characters, perhaps even inside your hero's head.

So how do we induce the Dream State? We must build it for our readers. There are basic building blocks, but, rather than big things, they are small things: tiny details.

Here's an excerpt from one of my short stories:

Lifting his cup, Everett shook his head and let the steam wash over his face, inhaling the earthy, bitter coffee scent. "Coffee's not much of a drink, is it?" he observed.

"It's comfortable," the old man said.

"What's that supposed to mean?"

"It's not supposed to mean anything; it's just true."

Everett sucked lightly at his cup, testing. "Still too hot. I should tell Marti to turn down the heat on that pot before they get a lawsuit from some jerk who spills on himself."

"Never happen," the old man said. He ran his thumb around the rim of his cup. "Look around you. Folks in here like their coffee hot, hot enough to have to wait for it to cool while they chew over their morning. Folks who come here don't sue when they spill coffee; they apologize and wait for Marti to bring napkins and a refill. Folks who sue for their own mistakes don't come here; it's too honest for them."

Notice the little details: the steam washing over Everett's face, Everett sucks at his coffee to test the heat, the old man absently running his thumb around his cup, the earthy scent of coffee, the coffee is too hot. I chose those details because they are common sights, smells, sensations, and experiences for nearly every reader. The readers already have those things swimming around inside their heads, and I am only twitching at them with my word-lures to get them hooked into my story. Tell me you didn't imagine a fish just then. You see how effective the right word choices are?

Give your reader tiny little details, little pictures, sounds, smells, textures, and tastes that they already have inside them, and then get them to relate those things to moments in your story that feel familiar and they will go into the Dream State without even noticing when it happens. And that's at the heart of inducing the Dream State: subtle, quiet touches.

Some of you may question the familiarity to be found in a fantasy or science fiction novel. Rest assured, while the tools, creatures, and landscapes in your tale may be new and unfamiliar, the heart of any story is the characters, and whatever facet of the human condition gets explored through your heroes, it will be familiar ground. All individuals, real or imagined, want to live, to find love, to succeed in their endeavors, and it is in the struggle to achieve these goals that readers will identify with your heroes. The personal doubts, the failings, the insecurities, the fears, and the inner obstacles all heroes must deal with go far beyond the setting and genre, for they are truly universal in scope. Everyone relates to the inner struggle, and all that remains is to flesh out the little details of place, setting, mannerisms, and speech patterns to give the reader full immersion in the Dream State.

One caveat: Never, *ever,* write a description that rambles on beyond the readers' attention span. There are a lot of writers out there who won't use one word where a thousand will do. And, with very few exceptions, they are completely forgettable. Pardon my language, but I call these writers *word whores*, because they write as if they are getting paid by the word. The late Robert Jordon, God rest his soul, was one of the worst offenders. Have you read his *Wheel of Time* series? Great story, but it moves at a glacial pace because his descriptions go on forever. In his second or third book in that series he describes a jacket worn by his hero. The description covers the better part of three pages. Three freaking pages! It's a *jacket*! You get the idea that it is a very cool, very fancy jacket inside of the first two sentences. Remember when I said subtle, quiet touches? Three pages is a two-by-four to the face that will drub the reader nigh into unconsciousness!

Look, if you want to jerk someone out of the Dream State, drone on about whatever you're describing until they have to drink an espresso to keep themselves awake long enough to get through it. Quick, short descriptions are key to maintaining the Dream State. The only time a description should go beyond two or three sentences is when you are setting a scene, or describing a major character. Also, awkward wording or confusing metaphors in such descriptions will further ruin the Dream State. Read your work aloud to be certain.

Quick summary: The foundations of the Dream State are set in tiny details that engage the imagination by calling up common life experiences. Don't go overboard.

ALL FIVE SENSES

As a beginning writer, I repeatedly made one of the most common mistakes; I only wrote with two senses—sight and sound. I did an excellent job of writing about what my characters heard and saw, but I never included what odors they smelled, textures they felt, or flavors they tasted. As you can imagine, this left my stories with a very flat and two dimensional feel.

Dream State arises from sensory immersion, and you cannot fully give the readers such an experience if you don't feed them sights, sounds, smells, tastes, and textures. You don't have to give them all five senses in every paragraph, but you should try to put at least four on every page. For example, every building has its own unique odor, even new buildings smell of fresh paint and sawdust. You can write about such odors as characters enter and leave homes and businesses. Everything solid has a texture that can be mentioned in passing as a character handles an object. Your characters must eat to live, so give their meals flavor. Indeed, you can include all five senses in a meal, for food is valued for its look, smell, flavor, texture, and even sound—celery would be nasty if it didn't crunch as you bit into it.

Think about using the senses to intensify conflict in a scene. How much worse is a fight if the enemy is ugly? If he stinks of sour urine? If his skin feels slick with sweat and grime? If he has a low guttural laugh? If your hero tastes coppery blood in his mouth and feels searing pain from a broken tooth?

The senses are often used to set mood. Entering a building made of rough-hewn wood denotes a primitive structure, and sets the scene for an encounter with someone who is rough and primitive in nature. Unpleasant smells usually are used to foreshadow an unpleasant event. A box of sweets on a table is often an indicator of friendly or romantic environs.

To get used to writing about more than just sight and sound you can try a simple exercise: Imagine you are blind. Now imagine you have just come awake in an eerily silent room and you are not in your own bed. Now write a page or two on how you would figure out where you are, and, being alone, how you would provide for yourself. You will have to use *all* of your remaining senses.

I recently had someone note that I am the only male writer he's ever read that includes odors in descriptions. I was surprised at this comment, partly because I hadn't noticed which genders wrote smelly descriptions, but mainly because it had been picked up on. It just goes to show that the reader is often far more conscious of the little details than you expect them to be. You need to be sensitive to readers' ability to absorb, sort, and appreciate all the information you throw at them. Being aware of this will force you to write carefully, use well thought out descriptions, and include enough bits of sensory input

for the readers to seize upon and build the Dream
State.

WHERE IDEAS COME FROM

This is actually a very common problem with writers of all experience levels: You settle down in front of your computer, poise your fingers over the keyboard, and… nothing. Your brain locks up and is as blank as the screen before you. You had an idea, but it's gone. Poof! What are you to do?

Whatever you do, don't stay locked in your house, moping around.

When this happens to me, I go out people watching. I look for interesting passersby and describe them in my head. I sit at a table in the local diner and watch other patrons, searching for the odd pairing, and then I begin to ask questions. Why are they together? What would be the worst reason for why they're here? The strangest reason? What would make the whole thing awkward? What would make it sad? Or dangerous? How weird could it get? Who would be the worst person to see them together? Why? What likely problems might arise from this meeting? What would be the most unlikely problems? Who would be hurt?

The most important question is always *what if?* What if the bad/weird/worst/awkward thing happened? I believe the best stories come from asking the what if questions. One of my favorite stories I ever wrote came from asking, *what if.*

My dad once told me about the day his father lay dying in the hospital and the family got the dreaded call: "You'd better come now, he doesn't have long." My father told his mother and siblings to go on without him. Dad then told me he stayed behind to milk the cows and take care of the animals because he knew the hospitals always waited to call until it was too late; the policy makers at hospitals back then believed it would be too hard on family to be there as loved ones passed away.

After I heard this story, I asked myself *what if* the policy had changed without him knowing, and he could have been there at his father's side to say goodbye? This led to me asking *what if* a husband missed his wife's passing because he sent his child ahead while he stayed behind to take care of some meaningless chore? What impact would that have? What would that kind of guilt do to someone? My story, *Solitaire*, arose from those questions and it is now the centerpiece of my anthology, *Solitaire and Other Stories*.

Another story prompter involves a simple exercise: pick up a newspaper and read about a crime or accident, and then write about it from the perspective of one of the people involved. Then write it again from another person's viewpoint. Imagine writing about an accident from the perspective of the tow truck driver, or the ambulance medic.

I am somewhat puzzled by writers who tell me they have run out of story ideas. "Did you die?" I ask. At their startled look I will go on to explain that life is full of stories and all they have to do is go for a walk to run into dozens of ideas.

Stories are all around us. People tell great and small stories every day, and if you listen, you may find one that sparks an idea inside you. I suggest you write down the outlines of such stories; use a notebook, a phone app, a tablet, or even a napkin if you must. Just write them down and save them for those times when that blank screen and the evil blinking cursor are staring back at you. Then you can pull them out of your wallet, pocket, or purse, and start asking questions. Soon your fingers will be flying over the keyboard, and down the road someone will be asking you, "Where did that idea come from?"

START FIGHTING

You have finally come up with a great idea for a story, but you're not sure how to begin. That's easy; start with conflict. It's a cruel fact that you must capture your reader's attention within the first couple of pages if you expect them to buy your book. I say you must capture it in the first paragraph. I go further and say, do everything in your power to suck them in with your very first sentence. Start fighting; embroil your characters in battles—physical, mental, and emotional. In writer's terms this is called a hook. You want to hook the readers at the start of every chapter, and at the end of each chapter, so they are forced to turn the page just to see what happens next. If you ever get a letter from a fan telling you they stayed up all night reading your novel, then you'll know you've done it right.

The absolute best hooks involve conflict. Conflict consists of a desired outcome and an obstacle to that outcome. For example, your first sentence might be something like this:

Alice wondered how she might kill her boss without going to jail for murder.

Let's examine this sentence. Our main character has the desired outcome of seeing her boss dead. Okay, many of us can relate to that if we've ever had a boss that made us miserable, so we've set up a sympathetic character, and your reader is onboard with the whole dead boss thing. Now the obstacles show up, there is the moral issue of murder, and we don't want a character we're just starting to empathize with to actually cross that line; and then there is the whole police, court, prison issue riding close on the heels of the moral objections. Desired outcome running into opposition creates conflict, and conflict calls up questions in your readers' minds.

There are two things you want going on in your readers' minds at all times: Questions, and Dream State.

A question, curiosity, the natural inquisitiveness of humans is what keeps a person reading, delving deeper into a story. Conflicts cause questions like these to arise: What caused the conflict? How will the hero resolve the conflict? Will something occur to worsen the conflict?

Let's look at Alice's conflict again. If we follow the first sentence with something that shows Alice to be a spiteful, poisonous person just trying to get her boss's corner office, we will lose the readers' connection to our hero. The sense of conflict will diminish drastically with that connection loss.

However, what if the following lines lead us to discover Alice and her boss are in the executive washroom, and she has his penis in her mouth because he is blackmailing her into giving him oral sex every week in order to keep her fabulous job and the medical benefits that go with it? And then we learn Alice has a chronically ill son under a very expensive doctor's care… then she becomes a serious victim and we can relate even more to her desire for the man's death, and the conflict just went up to a whole new level for the readers. They now want exactly what Alice wants, and they really want to know how she's going to do away with the bastard. It has become real for them, and they are flooded with questions: How did Alice get in this predicament? Why doesn't she just go to the police and press charges? Could she go to Human Resources? Why doesn't she quit? How sick is her son? How will she kill the boss? How will she hide her involvement? What blackmail information does her boss have on her?

This is the type of conflict you want to start your story with. It doesn't need to be as gritty and dramatic as Alice's situation, but it does need to generate questions. Whether you start with a warrior fighting for his life, or a child hiding under the bed, the goal is to get your readers to ask questions that can only be answered if they keep turning pages.

This applies in biographies, histories, and true crime novels as well. Every life, every major event has an element of conflict. The secret is to find those conflicts and choose a good one to start with. Then take that conflict and give it to the readers in a way that is uniquely yours.

The best definition of conflict I've ever heard is the one Jerry Cleaver uses in his book, *Immediate Fiction*: Want + Obstacle = Conflict. Make your hero want something, throw an obstacle in his way, and now you've got conflict.

As you progress through your novel, each chapter will have fluctuating degrees of tension, but no chapter should be completely devoid of conflict as that is what drives a story. People read to immerse themselves in conflict resolution, to see triumphs, tragedies, and glories they cannot see in day to day life. Reading is every bit the escapism that watching

TV is, and, like TV, the more trouble you put your heroes in, the better ratings you will get. And the sooner you start putting them in trouble, the more firmly your readers will be hooked.

DIALOGUE: WHAT TO SAY?

Dialogue offers the writer a great many opportunities to develop both characters and plotlines. Dialogue, unfortunately, is often used to plop down great chunks of expository language, such as:

"Dear sister of mine, Agnes, you did hear that Jack and I, Norma, are getting back together after our long separation caused by the sudden drowning death of our third son, Bobby, for which Jack has never forgiven me even though I am blameless. Of course I resented such treatment even though deep down inside I knew I should have been paying closer attention to Bobby, who was in the swimming pool, instead of fussing so much over Timmy, my illegitimate fourth son from the time I had an affair with Joe, Jack's best friend from childhood."

When a reader encounters such a ponderous and messy piece of dialogue they don't feel better informed: they feel cheated! Dialogue is not intended to hand out information on a platter; it is intended to guide the reader toward conclusions. Remember that the speaking character has an audience that usually knows something about them—people seldom spill their life story to strangers.   Here's how the above dialogue could have been better handled:

"Jack and I are getting back together, Agnes."

"Really? You've been apart for what, two, three...?"

"Four years."

"So long? Has he finally forgiven you?"

"I don't know... he says so. I'm not sure I've forgiven myself."

"It wasn't your fault, Norma. Bobby knew better than to play in the pool without his brothers there."

"I still should have known where he was! If only..."

"What?"

"I was playing with Timmy, and I should have had all the boys with me. Maybe then... Oh, I don't know!"

"Timmy. Does Jack suspect yet?"

"No."

"Are you going to tell him?"

"I can't—he and Joe have been friends since fourth grade."

"Timmy looks more like Joe every time I see him. How long do you think it will be before Jack begins to see the resemblance?"

"I don't know. Let's change the subject, please. You really need to visit us—the boys miss their aunt something terrible."

This version took 66 words longer to write, but don't you feel like you have a clearer picture of who Norma is? Do you feel more compassion for her? More disdain? Has she become someone you feel you might have met at one time or another?

Now look over that last example of dialogue and see if you can find the word "drowned." How about "affair?" Or even "illegitimate?" "Guilt?"

None of those words are there, but the concepts are. Lead your readers to the conclusions you want them to make. By letting the readers make those conclusions on their own you allow them the opportunity to place themselves inside the character's head and *identify* with the character. Always give your readers a reason to identify with your heroes, and even your villains—it makes the reading a more personal, and thereby more enjoyable, experience.

Now let's talk about realism: This ain't the place for it.

Dialogue in fiction isn't meant to be real—it's meant to be better than real life! Your characters should speak the way you *wish* people would speak, with none of the "um...ah...like...you know!" vocal pauses found in the real world. Make your language beautiful! Read Ernest Hemingway's book, The Sun Also Rises. It's a masterpiece of dialogue and *nobody* ever spoke like his characters.

As an editor I've struggled through countless frustrating bits of dialogue that look something like this:

"Ah sho 'preshiates yo' gittin' me dis hyar job, Mistah Wilson."

When I asked the writers why they used such language the answer was always the same: "I wanted it to be realistic—to show that the character was an uneducated sharecropper from the Deep South."

Baloney! That is gimmicky dialogue intended to impress the reader with the writer's "authenticity." The same feel for accents can be given without the reader wondering where they left their Deep South Translation Book.   Here is an example of three distinctive "accents" from my novel, Aviara:

"The High Eyre Mountains ain't like these here mountains," said Becca. "Our lands is drier, colder and rockier. Oh, sure, these mountains is rocky, but you got more plants and trees here."

"I see," Aarn said excitedly. He'd pulled out a pen and parchment from his pack and wrote the answers to his questions down; his pen scratched furiously across the paper with each new insight. "Let me get this straight," he continued. "You come from a mountainous region with sparse vegetation; is that correct?"

"Is few plants, yes," agreed Rafe, happy that he'd understood the scholar for once.

From the scholarly language of Aarn to the Southwestern flair of Becca to the cropped speech of Rafe, these accents do not need the heavy-handed dialogue with all the punctuation marks; they simply need the suggestion of a theme, a characterization through dialogue. The better a character's education, the more they use what Hemingway referred to as the two-dollar words. Likewise, the lower the education, the shorter the words used in dialogue. Examples:

Execute = kill.

Terminate = end.

Imbibe = drink.

Elucidate = teach.

Pontificate = preach.

Grammar may also change with education:

I completed that = I done did that.

That wasn't proper = that weren't no way to did that.

Use your dialogue to suggest what you want the readers to know, rather than spelling it out for them. They will thank you for it. Remember, the effort you put into developing your dialogue is never wasted. Readers will be caught up right away if the dialogue draws them in and shows off your characters!

THE ACTIVE VOICE

What is meant by "voice?"

1. The style of narrative chosen by the author, i.e.; third person, first person, etcetera.

2. The technical aspects of the writer's prose; does the language flow? Is it easy to read?

3. The most common meaning is based on whether the language used is "active" or "passive." This is the aspect we'll deal with here.

Passive language is often expository in nature—an explanation of a situation or a mood. Common passive sentences are like these:

- John was tired enough to cry because he'd been working at the factory all day.
- Jennifer hated her neighbors because they were richer than her.

- Billy felt the world was unfair to him.
- Sally probably wouldn't make the swim team after her poor performance at the tryout.

A few indications of passive language are the use of words that end in 'ly', or the words *because, felt, seem*, or negative words in general; *not, can't,* and *won't* to name a few. These are often, but not always, signs of passive language.

The old writer's admonishment says, "Show, don't tell." *Showing* is simply the use of the active voice—phrasing what you want the reader to learn in such a way as to engage the imagination so that they *see* what you are telling them. Let's look again at our first passive sentence example:

John was tired enough to cry because he'd been working at the factory all day.

When you read that sentence do you *see* John? Do you *see* him as tired? No? Why not? BECAUSE THERE WAS NO NEED FOR YOUR IMAGINATION TO BE ENGAGED! You were *told* his circumstances; the conclusions were drawn out for you. The most important skill you can master as a writer is the art of leading readers to the right conclusions *without telling them*. It is the difference between being told that your dog was killed by a car, or being led to the side of the road and allowed to observe the corpse for yourself. Which method would have the greater impact? Which would be more *real* to you?

Active voice *demonstrates*. Think about times when you have been bone weary and ask yourself some questions.

- How did you move?
- What was your posture?
- What facial expressions did you wear?
- How quickly did you react to stimulus?
- What tones or inflections did your voice acquire or lose?

- What thoughts ran through your head?

Each of these symptoms are clues to set down on paper for that almighty detective—the reader.

Let's "show" John's situation in a more active way:

The evening whistle sounded at the plastics factory and workers spilled out, feet scuffing, shoulders slumped, and heads down as they trudged through the parking lot with dazed expressions, searching for their vehicles. John stepped out last, leaning back against the factory door to close it. He rested there a moment, lifting one callused hand to wipe the sweat from his face, then gathered his strength and stumbled toward his battered red pickup. He pulled himself into the cab and sat, staring at the gray factory building. *There went another ten hours sucked out of my life*, he thought, *and I'll lose ten more tomorrow.* His eyes blurred and John let his head go down against the cool plastic steering wheel as he wept.

Write events as if you were observing them and hand the spectacle to your readers in as unbiased a manner as possible. Give them the actions; the descriptions that they need to form a picture in their own mind. We are trying to induce a dreamlike state in their heads and they need imagery, not statements, in order to slip into your story. A statement like *Ed hated Marge* is fine only if you follow by supplying IMAGES to bring the imagination into play: Ed's hands must clench when Marge enters the room. The vein on the side of Ed's head should start throbbing when he hears Marge's voice. His body language should change when she's around. A leg twitch could be used to indicate his stress levels skyrocketing. Have fun with all the little ways you can *show* us what's going on in Ed's head.

The active voice is about demonstrating what is happening in a manner that engages the imagination, while the passive voice tells you what happens in a manner that is dry and uninspiring. Remember: Show, don't tell!

MYTHIC STRUCTURE IN MODERN WRITING

Mythic structure is the oldest form of story, and arguably the form that people best respond to. A few representatives of mythic structure in movies from recent times are The Matrix, the first Star Wars film, Disney's The Lion King, and the Harry Potter series— all excellent adventures that follow a hero's journey, which is the heart of mythic structure.

Dr. Joseph Campbell did years of research that culminated in an enlightening, but ponderous, book on mythic structure titled *The Hero with a Thousand Faces*. One of his students and a Hollywood movie consultant, Christopher Vogler, managed to condense it down to a more manageable book titled *The Writer's Journey: Mythic Structure for Writers*. Still, Vogler's book is a bit more than you may want to tackle in one sitting, so here's my brief overview:

Mythic structure is found in all the great legends of Greek, Celtic, and Norse mythology, and gave birth to ancient heroes in all lands and cultures of the world. This mythic structure is recognized as the shaping of a MC (main character) hero through an arduous journey to collect some much needed item or person and return safely home with said item/person, which prepares the hero to face the ultimate evil and return balance to their world.

The stages of the hero's journey:

1. Normal Life: The everyday hero at home. We get a feel for our MC's day-to-day routine, his social standing (often poor), and his family status.

2. Let's Do the Quest: An invitation to step through the looking glass. Something out of the norm occurs and the MC is given the chance to do something they might not be ready for. Think of the children stepping through the wardrobe in Chronicles of Narnia.

3. The Hero Says No: *Adventures? We don't need no stinking adventures*! Consider the MC hero to be a timid soul, not ready to step out of their comfort zone. Think of every movie where the hero keeps saying, "I just want to go back home."

4. I'll be Your Guide for This Part of the Trip: A mentor shows up to point the way. Think of King Arthur's Merlin, the most famous mentor of all time. Mentors show up just in time to give the MC hero a prod in the right direction.

5. The Going Gets Tough: The first obstacle appears and the hero has to commit himself to the quest thereby crossing a threshold into the wide wild world of adventure. In the Spiderman movies this is where Peter Parker deals with guilt over his Uncle's death and commits to fighting crime.

6. Lions and Tigers and Friends, Oh My: The hero gathers allies and begins to encounter the forces arrayed against him. I like the imagery of Robin Hood being declared outlaw by

Prince John, and going on to gather his band of merry men in the classic Errol Flynn movie— including his fights with Little John and Friar Tuck which turn enemies into allies.

7. Momma Told Me Not to Come: The hero has to cross a major threshold and enter a very dangerous situation to locate the object of the quest. Usually there is a gatekeeper here. Robin Hood risks the archery tournament held by Prince John for the opportunity to see his love, Maid Marion; the Sheriff of Nottingham is the gatekeeper.

8. I Have a Very Low Pain Threshold: The hero must endure a terrible ordeal (Usually, but not always, both mental and physical) in order to recover the quest item. In a war movie this is often where the beloved sergeant or captain is killed and it is up to the wounded hero to push on in spite of this loss and his personal injuries.

9. Gotcha! But Can I keep Ya?: The hero gets what he came for and starts (sometimes reluctantly) his return trip, often with trouble

hot on his heels. In westerns the cowboy has rescued the town girl from the gang of rustlers, but has to travel through the badlands that are full of angry Apaches while being pursued by Black Bart and his gunslingers.

10. I'm Born Again: The hero must internalize the lessons learned on the quest and shed the old persona for the new in order to return balance to the world—in a tragedy, this is where everything falls apart and the hero fails. The best example of this is in the first Star Wars movie where Luke fully trusts the Force and uses it to destroy the Death Star.

11. All's Well That Ends Well: The healing takes place. The lessons learned are shared—in a tragedy, the readers learn the lesson instead of the hero. I think a great example of this is the ending of It's a Wonderful Life where George Bailey runs home, happy to be in the town where he once felt trapped, finally understanding what a wonderful life he truly has and he shares that joy with his friends and

family as the community rallies around George in his hour of need.

The hero's journey is peopled with archetype characters: Hero, Mentor, Fool, Gatekeeper, Chameleon, and Dark Lord. If you've read the Harry Potter books you can easily spot these archetypes:

Hero = Harry Potter

Mentor = Professor Dumbledore

Fool = Ron Weasely

Gatekeeper = Professor Snapes

Chameleon = Hermione Granger (She puts on the appearance of several archetypes in each book, from mentor to fool and occasionally gatekeeper.)

Dark Lord = Voldemort

Use mythic structure as a guide, but not as a formula: Not everything you write will fit the mythic structure, nor should it!

CAUSE AND EFFECT

We need to discuss something that is a major source of annoyance to editors and readers everywhere. Cause and effect. Many new writers don't seem to understand the concept. Many ignore this common sense approach to writing and it shows up with glaring frequency.

Here is the gist of it: If a character does something, there needs to be a reason why. A sound, logical reason.

I cannot tell you how many times I have read a story submission where a soldier is walking through a war ravaged village and he suddenly dives through an open doorway spraying bullets everywhere. No reason for this action is given; apparently it's an open doorway and therefore needed someone to dive through it firing madly. There was no sudden movement in the doorway, no glint of a raised gun barrel, no shadow of a knife cast on the wall. In other words, there was no cause for the soldier to take that action. The writer's imagination may have held the threat, but unless it is passed along to the reader the result is a piece of writing that looks silly.

If a gun barrel had been glimpsed out of the corner of the soldier's eye, it would have been ample *cause* for an action. The *effect* would be the resulting diving and shooting. All very sound and logical.

This problem is seen often in bad movies and TV shows when a simple solution to a life threatening situation suddenly appears. A lever hitherto unnoticed opens an escape hatch. The ring that has been present on the sidekick's hand for the entire movie suddenly glows and is announced to be able to teleport them away from the otherwise insurmountable danger. These cheap and downright stupid solutions work against cause and effect.

If they had been searching for the ring because of its magical properties, then it might not be so bad if they found it and suddenly discovered the teleporting ability at the last second. The cause would be knowledge that it had some magic that might help, and the effect would be that they experimented until they discovered the teleporting ability.

I know inexplicable things happen in daily life, but they cannot happen in fiction. It's simply too unbelievable and it will hurt your story.

Ernest Hemingway said that he always tried to write stories that were "truer than true." This is what we all must strive for; to write fiction that feels more real than actual life. Every action, every event must have a reason for why it takes place. If things happen "somehow," or "someway," then your story is likely to be rejected, if not by an editor, then by your readers.

Oh, that soldier story I told you about? I really did get that submitted to me at an online magazine I worked for. I rejected it. But if it had been a comedy instead of a serious war story, and the Johnson family cat died in surprise amid a hail of bullets… that might have worked. Cause and effect can sometimes be suspended for humor, but only for a laugh!

MAKE THE STORY YOURS

When you write, bear in mind that this is *your* story. Every word of it belongs to you. Don't lose sight of that fact; it will empower your words. When you create a character, think about what will make that character yours and no one else's. What attribute can you give this character of yours that is completely different from any other author's? Does your character have a tiny puckered scar on the back of their thigh from when they were shot with a BB gun as a youngster by a neighborhood bully? Do they have an unreasoning fear of elderly women in black fur coats?

Part of bringing readers to the Dream State is giving them details they can latch onto, familiar objects, settings, and mannerisms that spring easily to mind. It is even more important that you give these details a tiny touch that is all yours. This is the little detail that engages the imagination and makes it work just hard enough to get the Dream State juices flowing and the mind stimulated, but not enough to cause confusion.

Do not go overboard with the details or you risk boring your readers. Think of details as seasoning, a little enhances the meal while too much makes it unpalatable. Compare these descriptions:

Bert picked up his belt and studied the scuffed creases where the buckle rubbed deep into the brown leather in daily use.

Bert picked up his belt and admired the shiny brass buckle with the deep scratch where he'd accidentally gouged it when he got in the knife fight with a Ugandan gambler down at Eddie's Bar in the small Texas town on the border of Mexico, near where Pancho Villa's banditos crossed the Rio Grande on their way home from raiding ranches in the early 1900's.

Okay, the second sentence has a lot more going on, but wasn't your brain spinning a bit as you read? That is exactly what you want to avoid. The first sentence isn't as exciting, but it gives little details that are easy to focus on: scuffed creases, rubbed deep, brown leather.

The information you give your readers needs to come in easy-to-swallow bites, not because the readers are stupid, but because the mind needs time to absorb and project the images upon the screen. Small bites are easier to digest and use. These are the foods of the Dream State.

Imagine you are at a banquet and the table is laden with hundreds of delicacies you've never tasted before. Now imagine the host demands that you eat an entire plateful of each item before you progress to the next. How long would it take before you'd gorged yourself? Two plates? Three? Four? What is certain, is that it wouldn't take long before you'd had enough and the banquet lost its allure. This is the risk we take as writers when we try to cram a hundred details down our readers' throats. Give them morsels. Let them have small tastes of your prose, give them a variety of phrasings, a dab of metaphor now and then, and they will love the feast that is your novel.

Now let's go back to our example sentences and break the details into small, digestible pieces:

Bert scooped his belt off the floor and studied the scuffed creases where the buckle rubbed deep into the brown leather in daily use. He grinned at the shiny brass buckle with the deep scratch. He'd accidentally gouged the buckle when he'd stumbled in a drunken bar fight and fell on his own knife, nearly impaling himself. Only the blade catching on the buckle had saved him from serious injury.

His opponent, a fierce looking Ugandan gambler easily as drunk as Bert, had found this hilarious and the fight ended with the two of them howling in laughter and staggering out of Eddie's Bar, arms around each other.

The locals had stared at the mad duo as they wove unsteadily through the streets of the small Texas community. They shook their heads and clucked their tongues; the border town hadn't seen such a disgraceful display since Pancho Villa's banditos passed through on their way to the Rio Grande in the early 1900's.

Do you see how the same information can be imparted, piecemeal, to create a broader picture? This version is broken into three paragraphs and took nearly a hundred words longer to write, but the pacing is slowed down to an acceptable level, and the story is fleshed out and made richer. The reader's head won't hurt from a huge dump of information in a tiny space of words.

A story should be structured out to be consumed at a leisurely pace, rather than fired at high velocity into a surprised brain. The reader has time to take in what you are feeding them, savor the flavors, and immerse themselves in the imagery. That is how you guide them into the Dream State.

The little details are what made the last description unique: A brass buckle with a scratch from a knife, a drunken brawl with a Ugandan gambler, and a town that had seen Pancho Villa. These are unusual details, they are not the cliché touches that are expected, and so put this story on a different level than the common. This is what you must do with every story you write; find little ways to make it uniquely yours.

REVISION

Revision is about two things, for the most part, and that is correcting word flow issues (things that make the reader stumble as they read), and reducing your writing down to only what is needed. Sure, you may have to clarify a statement here or there, and do a little fleshing out of your story, fix a few typos, but revision is predominately about cutting away anything that is unnecessary.

William Strunk wrote, "Vigorous writing is concise. A sentence should contain no unnecessary words, a paragraph no unnecessary sentences, for the same reason that a drawing should have no unnecessary lines and a machine no unnecessary parts." The first time I read that, it opened my eyes. My writing vastly improved once I understood that it wasn't about using as many words as possible, but only the ones that count.

A good exercise for this is to look at a page of your writing and see how close you can come to cutting the word count in half and still maintain the integrity of the story. An editor once asked me to reduce a 2000 word story down to 1200 words. I got it down to 1216 words before it was accepted, and it was a better story for it.

The other part is to try to make the language sing as you read it. Read everything you write out loud! If you stumble over the words, or run out of breath on a single sentence, then it's time to make some adjustments.

Remember, the sound of the language inside your reader's head is important. If the sound isn't flowing smoothly, then the dream state gets interrupted and the reader is annoyed. Too many annoyances and you've lost a reader, not just for this story, but all future ones as well.

Look at your storyline. As you go through your novel ask yourself if what you're reading moves the story forward. If it does, fine. If it doesn't, determine whether it adds enough to the story to make it worth keeping. Harden yourself to be ruthless with your words. You must be able to cut away any words, sentences, paragraphs, pages, and even chapters that don't move the story forward.

Imagine your storyline as a train taking your readers from one destination (the beginning) to another (the end). You want that trip to be as smooth as possible, with as few delays as you can manage. This will keep your passengers happy. Now imagine that each random tangent is a sidetrack that delays the train. Each overlong description is a crossing that slows the train down. Each pointless run of dialogue is an extra stop at an empty station for no reason. Enough of these delays will spoil the trip and cost you repeat riders.

Keep only what is absolutely necessary to get the passengers to the final destination, the last page in your book, and you will have plenty of repeat customers to ride along with you.

DON'T DO IT ALONE

As a rule, writing is a lonely profession. You sit alone with your thoughts, the cold silence, and the blank page before you. As you struggle to coax the muse into feeding you a few words in the proper order, there is no one at your shoulder helping to bear the burden of a creative block. Few of us have, or would want, someone to blot the sweat from our fevered brow when the creative juices are flowing out our pores. The isolation we write in is a necessary thing; for one word spoken aloud at the wrong moment could easily shatter that much needed trance we delve into during the creative process. I've lost whole paragraphs of (hypothetically) brilliant prose because someone poked their head into my office and asked if I knew where the TV remote was just as I finished composing the piece in my head, but before I'd actually typed it out.

However, once the first draft is done, you will need a support team. You are far too close to your project to judge it dispassionately. You will need first readers or some form of a critique group to give you honest feedback. If you plan to publish traditionally, you will need an agent to market your novel to a publisher. You will need an editor. If you are going through a publishing house the editor will be provided, but if you are e-pubbing you will need to find a freelance editor. You also need an artist to do your cover—again publishing houses provide those, but indie-pubbers are on their own. Formatting, line edits, marketing, and a host of other little details require other people be involved every step of the way in bringing your book to market.

As important as all the other professionals are to our publishing, I want to focus on the two groups of people most important to a writer: Family, and other writers.

Writers, as a whole, are an odd bunch. Many of us are filled with self-doubt and a host of other insecurities. Others are arrogant, brash, and have less than perfect social skills. Our families are both our support system and our buffer against the world at large. It is important that you include your family in the writing process—not in any professional capacity unless they actually *are* professionals—but as cheerleaders, confidants, and a source of comfort when things aren't going the way you hoped. It is all too easy to push family away when you want to write, but you must strike a balance as they are so important to a writer's life. Family members make the disappointments bearable, and the triumphs more joyous!

Writers need writers. Only another writer understands what you go through to produce a great piece. Whether they write fiction or news articles, every writer will know something you don't, and often are willing to share their knowledge and experience. And most importantly, they will understand exactly what you mean when you talk about writing. This is something that your family probably won't be able to help with; you need to talk to people who crawl out from under the same creative rock as you. It is such a comfort to know you're not the only one who suffers writer's block. It is so important to share your successes with your peers—even though we are all a little jealous of each other's triumphs.

I have been fortunate to have been mentored by many solid writers, my journalist mother foremost among them. I have always tried to be available to mentor other writers because I feel it would be a poor way to reward those who helped me if I did not pass along the lessons they shared so freely with me. It is my hope that you, too, will share the lessons learned in your writing life with those who are fledglings to this craft.

I always urge writers to join local writing clubs, online groups, and the professional organization affiliated with whatever genre is appropriate to their interest. I started out writing for children and so I joined the Society of Children's Book Writers & Illustrators (SCBWI).

A national organization usually will have regional and local meetings where you can get together with other writers to learn and share. I eagerly looked for information on local SCBWI meetings and discovered the closest was over an hour away from where I lived. I felt that was too far, and so I offered to start a local chapter and the regional head was tremendously supportive. Our first meeting had only three members in attendance, but grew over the years into about ten core members with others drifting in and out.

My point is this: if there are no writers' groups in your area, start one. I guarantee there are writers in your community who will want to join. I have started other writers' groups, and run many writers' workshops in the years since, and I have always found plenty of people hungry for the chance to connect with other writers.

Find a library, a bookstore, a restaurant with a private room, a community building, anyplace that will allow a small group to meet in a quiet place, and then ask the local paper to advertise your first meeting—most papers will list it in their community pages for free. Ask them to list it repeatedly in the weeks leading up to the first meeting, and then a couple of times before each monthly meeting.

If you want to start such a group, but don't know how you would run one, you can do what I do. The way I have conducted every first meeting goes like this:

1. Open the meeting with a general greeting, and then introduce myself, listing my credentials.
2. Ask everyone to introduce themselves and speak briefly about their writing and what they hope to get out of the group.
3. Mention any writing conferences, news, or publishing trends that may be of interest to the group.
4. Give a one paragraph writing assignment to describe a favorite room,

past or present—it's due at the start of the next meeting. This assignment gives everyone a chance to show exactly where they are in their writing skills.

5. Do a question and answer session where people can ask for writing tips, marketing suggestions, and discuss aspects of the writing life.

6. Ask people to bring a favorite book on writing to share at the next meeting— I've found some great books this way!

7. Close the meeting with an open invitation to get coffee at a nearby location immediately following the meeting. This is how you build a relaxed and friendly group that will last for years.

At the follow up meetings, I follow this program:

1. Open the meeting with a general greeting.
2. Take note of visitors/new members and ask them to talk about their writing and what they want to get out of the group.
3. Discuss writing news, events, conferences, competitions, and any group plans for future events such as holiday parties.
4. Everyone reads their assignment out loud, and the group critiques it. This is easiest if everyone brings multiple copies to hand out for people to make notes on. If anyone has public speaking jitters, they can let another member read it out loud for them. Note: I ask that everyone give at least an equal number of positive comments for each critical observation, and nobody is to be outright cruel. I strictly limit critical comments to one or two per person, while positive comments are unlimited.

5. A general discussion period for all things writing.

6. Give a new one page assignment. I focus on assignments dealing with different aspects of writing: a page of dialogue between two characters, introduce a villain, fear, death, joy, love, smells, textures, opening paragraphs, hooks, holiday themes, etcetera.

7. Close the meeting and go for coffee with whoever has the time.

This is a proven, repeatable formula that you can use over and over again.

Again, this is all about building a support group for writers, because we all need people in our lives who can truly understand the joys and frustrations a writer deals with. To not have this support in place will make your growth as a writer much more difficult, and a great deal slower. It is only through feedback that we discover our writing strengths and weaknesses. It is only through the encouragement of our peers that we sustain our drive to succeed in the face of repeated rejections.

Just a final note: almost without exception, every writer I have met who sneered at writing groups and isolated themselves from other writers, were unsuccessful. Their writing progressed only so far, and then their skills stagnated. Interaction and criticism is only a small part of the growth cycle of writing; teaching is the other. As we grow, we may become a better writer than others in our writing group, but learning to guide those at the beginning of their writing career forces us to think through the creative process in ways that pull at your muse. I always say that I have learned far more by teaching a workshop than I ever did by attending one.

PUBLISHING

This is going to be a touchy subject, and many of you will not share my views on publishing. I will not say that you should follow my path, but I do hope you will prepare an open mind for what I am about to tell you.

You don't need a publisher.

Okay, now that you've had a moment to let that blasphemy sink in, let me explain my reasoning. Today, thanks to Kindle, Nook, Smashwords and the proliferation of the digital reader, we writers no longer are slaves to the Big Six publishing houses. When I started to write the only way to seriously think about publishing was to find an agent, who had you revise your novel, who then showed it to editors, who rejected it, and you started over with your next book. All too often, if an editor actually liked your manuscript, it would need to go before an editorial roundtable where the editor who liked your story had to pitch it to all the other editors, plus the marketing department. If only *one* of these individuals rejected your novel it did not get published. I had that happen—the marketing department at HarperCollins declined and said my story, *Man of Leaves*, was too quiet. I asked my agent if that meant I needed to give my characters grenades.

Many writers still feel as though traditional publishing is the only avenue for them because they will not feel validated unless a "real" publisher accepts their work. You may be one of these.

For me it's a different story: I am a journalist and an editor. Writing is my profession, I have been published many times, and people seem to like my style. I feel the only validation I need does not come from a marketing department, but from readers. I believe that is a sound viewpoint.

Look at how many independent authors have self-published, gone on to amazing success, and are now revered as great authors: Mark Twain, Upton

Sinclair, Gertrude Stein, Alexandre Dumas, James Joyce, Ezra Pound, Henry David Thoreau, Virginia Wolfe, Walt Whitman, E. E. Cummings, and Carl Sandburg just to name a few.

Consider the incredible success of *Fifty Shades of Grey* by E L James. James started out writing *Twilight* fan fiction and those stories evolved into the Grey series which she indie published and the series has gone on to become the fastest selling series in paperback history—faster even than JK Rowling's Harry Potter series—and has netted over $95 million to James including $5 million for the movie rights.

The traditional publishing houses have been very slow to adapt to the digital age, and their tactics show it. Most of the big publishers require the same price point on digital copies of their authors' books as on the paperback and hardcover copies. This is bad news for a new author since the production cost of a digital book after initial formatting and cover design is nonexistent and the buyers know it. The best information we have to date on price point for ebooks says the vast majority of readers buy at $4.99 or less.

When you look at the contracts traditional publishers use, you will find that authors are locked in at around 17% royalty from the digital list price, which the publisher often sets at $8.99. So with a list of $8.99, your royalty will be $1.53 per book. Happy with that? Uh, oh, I forgot… your agent gets 15%. Your actual royalty will be $1.30 per book, not that many will sell at the $8.99 price point...

Oh, and some of those contracts require you to grant all digital publishing rights to the house for the life of the copyright. Do you know what the life of a digital copyright is? Digital copyrights are good for the rest of the author's life, plus seventy years. In other words, some traditional publishers want to control all publishing decisions regarding your book for the rest of your life, all of your children's lives, and probably for the better part of your grandchildren's lives. That sounds fair, right?

Friends, writing is not only an art, it is also a business. You have every right to full control of your both your business and your art.

Let's take a second look at royalties. If you published independently with Kindle, for example, and you set your price point at the very attractive $2.99, you will qualify for a 70% royalty (minus a 2¢ delivery fee) that will total $2.08. Think about that for a moment; you saved your readers $6.00 and you made 78¢ more than if you'd published the traditional way. Plus, you retained full creative control of your book.

I understand there is still a little stigma attached to self-publishing, but it is fading away. Most of us remember when only the vain or untalented individuals self-published and we watched those poor artists with the hopeful expressions peddle their novels to local stores and libraries out of the trunks of their cars. We flinch inwardly when we think of following that path.

Now for the good news: the path has changed vastly. In the modern day there are quality online editorial services that will help you shape your novel into something you can really be proud of. Help is there for every step of the creation process; from plot issues, cover design, grammar and spelling edits, to marketing the final product.

Many honored authors are now eschewing the traditional path for epubbing because of both the financial and the creative rewards. Pulitzer Prize winning playwright and author David Mamet announced plans to self-publish this past April, 2013. This is no longer the shameful road once traveled only by the inept and the arrogant.

I will caution you, however, to wait until you have been published in several reputable magazines. This will let you know that you are writing at a professional level and your work will be of a quality that readers will appreciate. If you cannot get published in a magazine, then you should continue to write, read, and study the craft a little longer. Keep at it and your work will begin to gain acceptance letters, and then you will be able to self-publish with confidence.

WORKING THE WORDS

A writer's life is unlike any other; we are almost always alone during the creation process, yet we are always striving to connect with people in a deeply personal way. Nobody who hasn't struggled to work the words can ever understand the joy and pain of it. There are so many of us that would be better off if we walked away from that epic battle, but we just can't do it. One taste of putting together a truly beautiful sentence, and we are hooked forever.

There is a feeling of pressure in my head when I write, as though the effort is stretching my mind from the inside out. I love that feeling! I feel like a hero crushing my enemies as I cut away excess language to unleash the deep magic in a simple line of words.

I will not kid you; this is not an easy way to make a living. There will be weeks and even months when everything you write is lousy. Days when the words won't come, and your muse has posted a *gone fishing* sign over her usual spot on your shoulder. You will search for inspiration and find despair instead. If you don't threaten to quit the whole stinking business at least a handful of times along the way, then you aren't really trying.

Let's face it, folks—we're nuts! That's the only explanation for our endless compulsion to work the words. We belong in the asylum for the way we berate ourselves over a misplaced comma. The straitjacket should be employed to keep our hands away from that instrument of our self-abuse: the keyboard.

But, God, is this insanity beautiful or what? We just have to keep banging away at the keyboard—at the walls inside ourselves that keep the right words at bay. Once we learn the knack of keeping the muse lured close, and we start producing stories, poems, and novels that actually move people, then we discover a personal fulfillment beyond imagining.

The hardest part of working the words is the determination to keep learning, to continue developing your craft, to always strive to be unique, to constantly burn to write better than you ever have. That determination is exactly what is needed to write words worth reading, to stand out amid the sea of mediocrity that the world reads on a daily basis, and quickly forgets. Though it is difficult, such determination is the only thing which gives us the slightest chance of lasting beyond ourselves.

The digital medium assures our words will exist in cyberspace forever, but it is only the reading of those words that make them live. Homer is gone for over 2000 years, and yet we still read the Iliad and the Odyssey, and Homer breathes again as his words flare bright in our hearts and minds. Shakespeare still walks our stages and graces our ears with iambic pentameter nearly 400 years after his death. Hemingway's stories are taught in High Schools across America 50 years after his suicide.

There is one easy aspect of working the words, and that is reading. We have to read every day, for at least as long as we write, if not longer. Reading feeds the muse, enriches the vocabulary, and teaches us style and structure. We learn a lot from our competition. Reading also inspires us, if we read the right stories; the good ones.

I suggest that you read the acknowledged masters in whatever genre you wish to write in; there is a reason their work has lasted. Study them, and how they phrase things. There will be a unique feel to the way they write, and you want to develop a uniqueness of your own. I am not saying to copy these masters' styles, just to get a feel for them so that when you write you will be aware of what has been done before and you can avoid becoming cliché.

If you do not read poetry, I recommend that you begin now. There is a rhythm and flow to poetry, as well as graceful phrasing and metaphors, which inspire writers to use the language in new and beautiful ways. I have several collections by different poets that I go through, looking for a piece that catches my fancy, and a short half hour reading never fails to make the language sing in my head and my fingers itch for the feel of a keyboard beneath them. There are countless poetry sites online where you can go to read samples by a host of poets—new and old. Go find a few poets whose work speaks to you. Your writing will be the better for it.

Read essays on philosophy, history, politics, human behavior, and anything else you can find of interest. Such small doses of information will be useful when you are creating characters and putting them into interesting trouble. Just think how awkward a social gathering could become if your hero suddenly points out the error in the host's social pronouncements, historical observations, etcetera. Especially if the hero's boss is the host, and your hero has just embarrassed said boss in front of the entire office staff.

Read humor, it will help you when you need to lighten a scene. Besides, who couldn't use a laugh?

It may seem like I am suggesting you read everything. I'm not. Read as much and as widely as you can and still enjoy it. I promise you that very little of your reading will be wasted. I firmly believe knowledge is power, and if you intend to be a powerful writer, you will need to be a knowledgeable reader.

Working the words, once you've gained a measure of success, will throw a very troublesome thing in your path: ego. You will come to believe that you are as talented as the agents, editors, critics, and fans say you are. You will accept that you are a genius and launch into your next novel, shunning your support groups (critique group, family, first readers, etcetera), because you are obviously so brilliant you don't need them. You will be surprised at how easily the words come to you, and how wonderful the characters and plotlines are. You will finish your first draft glowing with the excitement of having produced the next world shaking novel. You are so confident in its perfection that you will submit it to your agent without changing a word.

"Is this a joke?" your agent asks in a testy phone call. "Did you really rewrite The Great Gatsby as a comedy? The *Mediocre* Gatsby? *Really?*"

"Ummm, yeah," you answer in confusion. Why can't your agent see the brilliance of the concept? "It's clever." You're surprised you need to point this out.

"It's ridiculous!" There is a deep sigh from the agent. "Have you got anything else?" You can hear the underlying tone that asks, *anything I wouldn't be embarrassed to show to a publisher?*

Our egos are powerful beasts that will drive us to do foolish things, if we let them. Never lose sight of the fact that we are only human, and we need help to achieve greatness. We need the help of others to point out the flaws in our work, whether it be grammar, punctuation, plot, story structure, or as basic as a bad idea for a book. We need to check our egos at the door when we step into our writing rooms and stare at the blank screen.

Ernest Hemingway, arguably the greatest writer of the twentieth century, once said, "I write 99 pages of shit for every one page of masterpiece. I try to leave the shit in the trashcan." If a master of the written word can acknowledge his ability to produce "99 pages of shit" on a regular basis, then how can we admit to less? Does any one of us dare to imagine that we are better than Hemingway?

It is that ever vigilant battle against ourselves that is the mark of a true writer. We are our own worst enemies in so many ways. We know we have something to say to the world at large, but we also struggle constantly to find the right words, and always feel that we are falling short. We understand the human condition and it kills us that when we try to share that understanding the words knot up inside us and won't come out with enough power to measure up to the agony and joy we see and feel so clearly.

Our insecurities surround and stifle us when we most need the inner strength to stand up and shout, "See! Do you see what is going on?!!"

Working the words is about conquering ourselves. We have to accept our failings, and yet believe in ourselves with enough conviction to keep writing, even when we know most of it will wind up in the trashcan. We have that power inside us. I promise you, if you look for it, if you keep stretching yourself, you will find it. The words will come. Little spurts of eloquence will rise up inside of you and you will be able say exactly the right words at the right moment and you will be able to fasten them to the page.

There will come a day, when you have fastened enough of the right words to the right pages, that you discover a completed, revised, edited, and incredible manuscript in your possession. You will be awed at what you have wrought. You will share this manuscript with others, and some of them will connect with it, and you will be awed all over again at that connection. On that day, you will truly know that you are, indeed, working the words!

And the world will be better for it.

ABOUT THE AUTHOR

Jeffrey Dean Doty grew up on a dairy farm in Northern Illinois. He began reading at an early age, and has held a lifelong love of the written word.

Jeffrey has two adult children, and still lives in Illinois with his beloved wife, Jean, and a fairly stable cat named Stella.

Jeffrey has published both fiction and nonfiction in national and regional magazines. This is his fourth book. He has taught writers' workshops, and mentored new writers for over fifteen years. Most of his students still like him.

Jeffrey encourages writers and readers with questions about writing to contact him at jeffdoty@hotmail.com . Please put the phrase *writing question* in the subject line. Please understand that Jeffrey only mentors a couple of writers each year, but he will do his best to answer questions in the order they are received.